Stories of Heart & Home

Compiled by Alice Gray

with paintings by Susan Mink Colclough

Multnomah Gifts™

Multnomah® Publishers *Sisters, Oregon*

Stories of Heart and Home
© 2002 by Multnomah Publishers, Inc.
Published by Multnomah Gifts™, a division of Multnomah Publishers, Inc.®
P.O. Box 1720, Sisters, Oregon 97759

ISBN 1-57673-948-1

Artwork © Arts Uniq'®, Inc.
Artwork designs by Susan Mink Colclough are reproduced under license from Arts Uniq'®, Inc.,
Cookeville, Tennessee, and may not be reproduced without permission. For information regarding
art prints featured in this book, please contact:

  Arts Uniq'®, Inc.
  P.O. Box 3085
  Cookeville, TN 38502
  1-800-223-5020

Designed by Koechel Peterson & Associates, Minneapolis, Minnesota

Multnomah Publishers, Inc., has made every effort to trace the ownership of all poems and quotes.
In the event of a question arising from the use of a poem or quote, we regret any error made and
will be pleased to make the necessary correction in future editions of this book.

Please see the acknowledgments at the back of the book for complete attributions for this material.

Scripture quotations are taken from *The Holy Bible*, New International Version ©1973, 1984 by
International Bible Society, used by permission of Zondervan Publishing House.

Printed in China

02 03 04 05 06 07 08—10 9 8 7 6 5 4 3 2 1 0

www.multnomahgifts.com

Table of Contents

Introduction: Whispers of Home by Alice Gray................................ 4

The Table by John V. A. Weaver................................ 7

Teacups of Love by Nancy Jo Sullivan................................ 13

Old Doors by Carla Muir................................ 17

A Single Crocus by Joan Wester Anderson................................ 19

The Spirit of Hospitality by Emilie Barnes................................ 25

A Light in the Window by Faith Andrews Bedford................................ 29

House on the Lake by Mike Royko................................ 37

Back Home by Emma Steward................................ 41

Porch Swing by Brenda A. Christensen................................ 47

This Is a Home Where Children Live by Judith Bond................................ 50

Lavender Memories by Sandra Picklesimer Aldrich and Bobbie Valentine....... 53

Nesting by Faith Andrews Bedford................................ 59

Gently Swinging by Kimber Annie Engstrom................................ 63

Leaving Home by John Trent................................ 65

Heritage of Faith by Sally J. Knower................................ 69

Homeward Journey by Janet Paschal................................ 77

Acknowledgments................................ 80

Whispers of Home

Alice Gray

Newly married and living in a tiny apartment in a crowded city, I dreamed of a romantic Victorian house with a rose-covered iron gate, elegant sitting room, and garden gazebo. These were the tomorrows I wove in my imagination as a young woman. Even now, I still think my old house of dreams would be a most charming place to live.

But as the years slipped by, I've learned that *today* is infinitely more important than any number of misty, imagined tomorrows. And I've come to understand that the sweet, simple pleasures of home are the real treasures after all.

Waking early to a robin's song.

Lingering over morning coffee.

The aroma of cinnamon rolls baking in the oven.

Sunbeams tracing lazy patterns in gold across the pages of my open Bible.

Good books spilling from overcrowded shelves.

A parade of favorite photographs across the mantel.

Newly opened flowers bursting with fragrance.

A gathering of family and friends.

Laughter filling the rooms.

The glow of lit candles as twilight gathers.

Relaxed conversation at the table after dinner.

An armchair by the fireside.

In the coming pages, I welcome you to sink back into the warmth of glowing hearth fires and moments of repose, of teacups and porch swings and well-used kitchen tables...to savor these glimpses of home and use their ideas to create some of your own.

Simple and lovely are the pleasures that ripple softly across my heart: they are the inexpressible joys that whisper, *Home*.

Ah! There is nothing like staying home, for real comfort.

JANE AUSTEN

The Table

John V. A. Weaver

No, it isn't much to look at. Just on old yellow oak table, I suppose you'd call it. It isn't that we couldn't have had mahogany or walnut, of course. Only—well, thirty-eight years sort of turns anything into a treasure.

It was Sam's father's wedding present to us. The table and six chairs—four plain-bottomed, two with leather seats.

I recollect as well as yesterday the first supper we ate at it. We had just come back from our honeymoon in Canada; it was a Monday afternoon. Sam had signed the lease on the little five-room house on Locust Street the week before the wedding.

During the entire month of honeymooning, while we were up there lazing around. fishing. and getting used to each other, I had been worried about what we were going to furnish the dining room with. I had been given a good deal of furniture from Mother, and Sam had moved some over from his flat, but neither of us owned a dining room table.

That trouble was settled the minute we entered the room and saw the yellow oak table, bright and shining, with a note from Father Graham on it.

I remember scrambling around to put some sort of a meal together—what it was doesn't matter. Pretty soon we were sitting in chairs at opposite ends. so close that we could touch hands.

Sam didn't pay much attention to the food. He kept looking at me—you know the way newlyweds go on. Then he said, "I guess you're about the prettiest girl anywhere, Mary. I'm glad this table is so short. It lets me see you all the better."

I had to laugh. "Why, silly," I answered, "it opens in the middle. There are extra leaves in the china closet. We can make it as long as we want!"

Looking a little sheepish, he glanced around at the four other chairs. Then he grinned. "Well," he said, "we'll be using those leaves before we're through, I reckon."

I couldn't half eat for laughing. Yes, and blushing, too.

See that whole row of round dents up next to my place? That's what Sallie did with her spoon. She was the only one that always hammered. She was our first.

Over there, right by the opening—that's where Sam Jr. tried to carve his initials once when he was about five. Sam caught him just as he was finishing the *s*. It was a warm night for one young man, I can tell you.

Of course we had put in one of the extra leaves a good many times before Ben came. The children were forever having friends over. Ben made the extra leaf permanent.

Then we commenced adding the second leaf. More friends, you see. I used to tell Sam, "You keep moving away from me."

He'd always answer the same thing.

"My eyesight's all right," he'd say. "I can see just as well how pretty you are." And he said it as if he meant it.

So the children grew up and the table grew to its longest. Sallie married Tom Thorpe when she was nineteen, and they lived with us for three years.

The boys were in high school then, and I tell you we made a big family. All three extra leaves hardly did. Sam at one end and me at the other. Ben and Sam Jr. and Sallie and Tom—and my first granddaughter, Irene, in her high chair.

But she had her place, too. By that time we were in the big house on Maple, and the noise, the life, the happiness! The table was certainly getting battle-scarred. Look at that burnt spot. That's where Senator Berkeley put his cigar down the night he stopped by.

Well, then Sam Jr. went off to college, and a little while after that Tom and Sallie set up housekeeping in their own home up on the Heights. So one of the leaves came out for good, and we didn't have so much use for the second, except for company once in a while.

It was quite a shock when Sam Jr. left college at the end of his third year and went out west to California. He didn't run off, you understand. We said he could go, although we were very disappointed he didn't stay and finish his education. But he was right. He has made a heap of money in real estate out there.

He comes back once a year for a week or so with Myra, that's his wife, and their two youngsters. Then the old table gets swollen back to its biggest. It seems mighty quiet when they go.

Ben came back and stayed with us two years after he graduated. We hoped he'd be content to settle down here in town for good, he was doing so well in life insurance. But that was just the trouble. The New York office wanted him, at twice the money, so he went. And the last leaf went out of the table with him.

That's been a year ago now. Sometimes I think of taking in a boarder. Not just any ragtag or bobtail; some nice young fellow who needs a good home. It's so quiet....

I said so to Sam the other night. "My goodness," I said, "the table's so little again. Why, you're right on top of me. You can see all my wrinkles."

Sam laughed, and then he put his hand out and squeezed mine. "My eyes have grown dim," he answered. "You look as beautiful to me as ever. I guess you're about the prettiest girl anywhere."

But still....

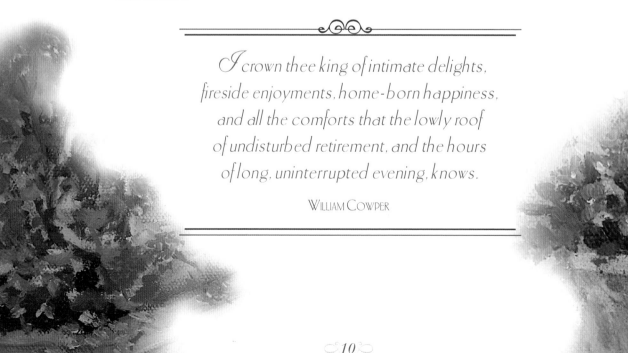

*I crown thee king of intimate delights,
fireside enjoyments, home-born happiness,
and all the comforts that the lowly roof
of undisturbed retirement, and the hours
of long, uninterrupted evening, knows.*

WILLIAM COWPER

Teacups of Love

Nancy Jo Sullivan

When I was a little girl, every Sunday was like a holiday. After church, my family—all eleven of us—would gather in my Grandmother Mema's kitchen. Wrapped in the aroma of warm cinnamon rolls and the sounds of small talk and percolating coffee, Mema would make her rounds, hugging us tightly, one by one, as if she hadn't seen us in years. Soon aunts and uncles and countless cousins would arrive. Everyone loved Mema.

One Sunday morning when I was about nine years old, Mema's kitchen got a little crowded. I slipped away from the congestion into Mema's dining room. It was a much quieter place, where warm sunlight streamed through paned picture windows and gilded rose prints adorned the walls.

Next to a drop-leaf table was a china hutch filled with polished teacups. During the hard years of the Great Depression, Mema had received each cup as a secondhand gift from a friend or relative. "They're cups of love…priceless," Mema used to say.

That morning I found myself admiring the porcelain patterns of the keepsake cups: every petaled rose, each silver-lined heart, every spray of emerald ivy. "Someday I'll collect teacups," I told myself as I pressed my hands against the glass doors of the hutch.

Mema peeked in on me from the kitchen. Drawing near, she saw me studying her collection.

"Which one do you like best?" she asked, smile wrinkles framing her cocoa-brown eyes.

"That one!" I pointed to a cup. It was lavender, decorated with gold leaves.

Sixteen years later, on my wedding day, I opened a small package that Mema had wrapped in white paper. Underneath a lacy bow, she had tucked in a card. "Your Favorite," it read. As I held the gift in my hand, I knew it would be the first teacup in my collection.

The early years of my marriage passed quickly. My husband and I didn't have much money, but I could always manage a few dollars for the teacup I found hidden behind the chipped punch bowl or the worn Tupperware at a garage sale.

By the time my second child arrived, I had scraped the peeling paint from an old glass-doored cabinet, refinishing it with a coat of maple stain. Now that I had a "hutch" of my own, I began to fill each shelf with my secondhand teacups. I placed Mema's wedding gift cup in the middle of the collection—it would always remain my favorite.

But while I was adding cups to my hutch, Mema was giving hers away. She was growing older and weaker from the cancer invading her bones. Nonetheless, she made sure that each of her keepsake cups found a home.

Like me, each of my sisters received one on her wedding day. So did the brides of my brothers and cousins. Every grandchild was given a "cup of love."

A few weeks after my third child was born, Mema's health began to worsen.

I visited her one last time while my husband watched the kids. Before I reached the bedroom where she lay, I passed through her dining room. Stopping for a moment, I pressed my hands against the glass doors of the hutch and peered inside. All of the cups were gone; only lines of sunlight filled the shelves.

Moments later, I sat at her bedside. "Mema," I whispered. "Your teacups…were they hard to give away?"

Mema took my hand. Though her breathing was labored, her eyes were warm and brown and bright.

"They were cups of love…and love is meant to be shared," she whispered. As Mema drifted off to sleep, I closed my eyes. A clear and lovely image was taking form in my memory.

Mema's life was like a beautifully patterned teacup, brimming with unforgettable tenderness, given to our family as a gift. She was a keepsake passed down to us from God, ours to cherish deeply, ours to admire forever in the hutches of our hearts.

A few years have passed since Mema died. I miss her, but my three young daughters remind me that she is never really far away.

Recently, on a sunlit Sunday morning, I watched them study my array of keepsake cups.

Together, they memorized the porcelain patterns: every petaled rose, each silver-lined heart, every spray of emerald ivy.

"Which one do you like best?" I asked Rachael, my youngest.

She pointed to a lavender cup, decorated with golden leaves. "That one!"

By wisdom a house is built,
and through understanding it is established;
through knowledge its rooms are filled
with rare and beautiful treasures.

PROVERBS 24:3–4

Old Doors

Carla Muir

The auction at a quaint old farm
brought many folks that day.
Most items sold for less than half
of what we thought we'd pay.
New owners did not care for old.
So on that day in June,
disinterested, they watched the sale
until the afternoon.
Then as the dusk of evening summoned
farmers to their chores—
the auctioneer began his bid
on beautiful old doors.
The bidding started at a price
below what they appraise.
But every time I gave my bid—
a frail, worn hand would raise.
So back and forth we both would bid
past what I could afford.
Although I wanted those old doors,
I stopped when prices soared.
Then as the sale reached closing time
and I began to leave,
I met the frail old woman with
the doors she did retrieve.
"Why did you pay so much for them?"
Her answer was precise:
"My children's heights are on those doors—
for which there is no price."

A Single Crocus

Joan Wester Anderson

It was an autumn morning shortly after my husband and I moved into our first house. Our children were upstairs unpacking, and I was looking out the window at my father, who was moving around mysteriously on the front lawn. My parents lived nearby, and Dad had visited us several times already. "What are you doing out there?" I called to him.

He looked up, smiling. "I'm making you a surprise." Knowing my father the way I did, the "surprise" could be just about anything. When we were kids, he once rigged up a jungle gym out of wheels and pulleys. A self-employed jobber, he was always building things out of odds and ends. For one of my Halloween parties, he created an electric pumpkin and mounted it on a broomstick. As guests came to our door, he would light the pumpkin and have it pop out in front of them from behind the bushes.

Today, however, Dad would say no more. As I became caught up in the busyness of our new life, I eventually forgot about his surprise.

That is, until one raw day the following March when I glanced out the window. Dismal. Overcast. Little piles of dirty snow still stubbornly littering the lawn. Would winter ever end?

And yet…was it a mirage? I strained to see what looked like something pink, miraculously peeking out from beneath a drift. And was that a dot of blue across the yard, a small note of optimism in this gloomy expanse? I grabbed my coat and headed outside for a closer look.

They were crocuses, scattered whimsically throughout the expanse of the front lawn. Lavender, blue, yellow, and my favorite, pink—little, bright faces bobbing in the bitter wind.

Dad. I smiled, realizing he had secretly planted the bulbs last fall. He knew how the darkness and dreariness of winter always got me down. What could have been more perfectly attuned to my needs? How blessed I was, not only for the flowers, but for his love.

My father's crocuses bloomed each spring for the next four or five seasons, bringing that same assurance every time they arrived: *Hard times almost over. Hold on, keep going, light is coming soon.*

Then came a spring with only half the usual blooms, and the next spring there were none. I missed the crocuses, but my life was busier than ever. Besides, I had never been much of a gardener. I thought I would ask Dad to come over and plant new bulbs. But I never did.

He died suddenly, one gray October day. My family grieved deeply, leaning on our faith. I missed him terribly, though I knew he would always be a part of us.

Four years passed, and on a dismal spring afternoon I was running errands and found myself feeling depressed. *You've got the winter blahs again,* I told myself. *You get them every year; it's chemistry.* But it was something else, too.

It was Dad's birthday, and I

found myself thinking about him. This was not unusual—my family often talked about him, how he had lived his faith. Once I saw him take off his coat and give it to a homeless man. Often he'd chat with strangers passing by his storefront, and if he learned they were poor and hungry, he would invite them home for a meal. But now, in the car, I couldn't help wondering, How is he now? Where is he? Is there really a heaven?

I felt guilty for having doubts. *But sometimes,* I thought as I turned into our driveway, *faith is so hard.*

Suddenly I slowed, stopped, and stared at the lawn. Muddy grass and small gray mounds of melting snow. And there, bravely waving in the wind, was one pink crocus.

How could a flower have bloomed from a bulb more than eighteen years old, one that had not blossomed in over a decade? But there was the proof. Tears filled my eyes as I realized the significance of that single crocus. *Hold on, keep going, light is coming soon.*

The pink crocus bloomed for only a day. But it built my faith for a lifetime.

The Crocus

Down in my solitude under the snow,
Where nothing cheering can reach me,
Here, without light to see how to grow,
I'll trust nature to teach me.

From my heart will young buds diverge,
As rays of the sun form their focus;
And I from the darkness of earth shall emerge
A happy and beautiful crocus!

Gaily arrayed in my pink and green,
When to their view I have risen,
Will they not wonder how one so serene
Came from so dismal a prison?

Many, perhaps, from so simple a flower
This useful lesson may borrow,
Patient today through its gloomiest hour,
We come out the brighter tomorrow.

Hannah F. Gould

The Spirit of Hospitality

Emilie Barnes

My mother's parlor was tiny, just an extra room behind the store. But her tablecloth was spotless, her candles glowing, her flowers fresh-cut, her tea fragrant. Most of all, her smile was genuine and welcoming whenever my mother invited people to "come on back for a cup of tea."

How often I heard her say those words while I was growing up. And how little I realized the mark they would make on me.

Those were hard years after my father died, when Mama and I shared three rooms behind her little dress shop. Mama waited on the customers, did alterations, and worked on the books until late at night. I kept house—planning and shopping for meals, cooking, cleaning, doing laundry—while going to school and learning the dress business as well.

Sometimes I felt like Cinderella—work, work, work. And the little girl in me longed for a Prince Charming to carry me away to his castle. There I would preside over a grand and immaculate household and be waited on hand and foot by attentive servants. I would wear gorgeous dresses and entertain kings and queens who marveled at my beauty and wisdom and brought me lavish gifts.

But in the meantime, of course, I had work to do. And although I didn't know it, I was already receiving a gift more precious than any dream castle could be. For unlike Cinderella, I lived with a loving Mama who understood the true meaning of sharing and joy—a Mama who brightened people's lives with her spirit of hospitality.

Our customers quickly learned that Mama offered a sympathetic ear as well as elegant clothes and impeccable service. Often they ended up sharing their hurts and problems with her. And then, inevitably, would come the invitation: "Let me make you a cup of tea." She would usher our guests back to our main room, which served as a living room by day and a bedroom by night. Quickly a fresh cloth was slipped on the table, a candle lit, fresh flowers set out, and the teapot heated. If we had them, she would pull out cookies or a loaf of banana bread. There was never anything fancy, but the gift of her caring warmed many a heart on a cold night.

My Mama's willingness to open her life to others—to share her home, her food, and her love—was truly a royal gift. She passed it along to me, and I have had the privilege of passing it on to others. What a joy to be part of the spirit of hospitality!

The little things we do at home,
like putting wildflowers in a vase,
are invisible medicine for all the bumps
and bruises of family life.

KATHERINE STEWARD

A Light in the Window

Faith Andrews Bedford

Moving day was drawing to a close. The van rumbled off down the lane, leaving us with three hungry children, a frightened cat, and a mountain of boxes to unpack. Our new home seemed vacant and lonely; the nearest neighbor was about a mile down the road. I could see a faint light glimmering through the woods.

Presently I heard the crunch of tires on gravel; a small pickup truck pulled in beside the barn. When I opened the door, I was greeted by a warm smile. Our new neighbor, Marian, had brought us dinner, friendship, and advice.

My little red address book, full of all the names and numbers a family needs to function, was of no use in this new place. I peppered Marian with questions: Who was a good vet? Where could I find aged manure for the garden? Was there a good plumber in town?

I learned with dismay that the nearest dentist was thirty miles away. But Marian assured me that the drive was beautiful.

She was right. As we drove through the valley, the hills were ablaze with autumn colors. Sugar maples bordered the old stone walls and yellow willows hung suspended over the stream that meandered alongside the road. In the golden meadows, cows grazed contentedly. We all decided that our favorites were the belted Galloways; their wide band of white in the middle of their black bodies made one think of Oreo cookies.

By the time we left Dr. Thomasson's office, dusk was beginning to settle. As we passed the edge of town, Drew asked, "Why does each house have a Christmas candle in the window when it isn't even Halloween?"

I remembered that the Syndersville Apple Festival was slated for the coming weekend; we had planned to help with the cider pressing. Perhaps this was some sort of tradition, part of the festivities.

That evening, when I called the cat in, she did not come. Kate had been confused ever since the move, meowing forlornly as she wandered through the unfamiliar house. The following morning she was still missing.

Then winter closed in. The children worried about Kate, and I tried to reassure them that she had probably found a nice warm barn to stay in for the winter. She was hibernating, I said, like a bear.

Mud season delayed the plowing. Spring chores piled up. Finally one warm March afternoon as the first daffodils were blooming, the children and I headed back to Syndersville to buy new shoes. Sarah couldn't decide between the red sneakers or the white, and Eleanor took a long time finding the right pair of party shoes. It was late by the time we left for home. Dusk was beginning to fall.

"Look," said Eleanor as we neared the outskirts of the village, "those houses still have lights in the windows."

We saw that the windows of four or five

houses on the left side of the road and three on the right each held a single lit candle.

I asked Marian if she knew why, and she answered simply, "It's the way it's always been." Then she laughed. "That's a common answer to a lot of questions around here."

The following month, while the children were being seen by Dr. Thomasson, I asked his nurse if she knew the answer to the mystery.

She just shrugged and replied, "That's the way it has always been."

I hid a small smile.

"Excuse me," a voice behind me said. I turned around. An elderly lady in a green print dress motioned to me from a sofa in the waiting room.

"Come sit by me," she said, patting the seat beside her. "I'd be happy to tell you about those candles. I'm Grace Harding, and I live in the last house on the left. You know, the little red one?"

"Yes," I said. "I admired your beautiful forsythia on the way into town."

"Forty years ago, when I married Henry and came to Syndersville, the first people to welcome us were the Johnsons, Clem and Anna. They lived in the farmhouse set back from the road."

I had seen the neat, white frame building set among its barns and outbuildings. It looked sort of like a mother hen surrounded by her chicks.

"They had two sons: Arthur, the elder, a strong, helpful boy who took after his father; and James, a quiet sort. He liked to read books. He's a professor over at the state college now." She smiled at Sarah, who was sitting beside me, listening intently. "When we began to have children, their daughter, Mary, used to mind them when we went to the cinema.

"Well, the war came along and Arthur signed up. It nearly tore Anna apart, him being her firstborn and all. But he wouldn't be dissuaded. James stayed home and helped his father run the farm." She sighed. "A lot of the village boys went off to war." For a moment, she seemed lost in recollection.

Drawing herself back to her story, she continued. "Arthur wrote home regularly, and Anna used to read his letters to all the neighbors. She was very proud of him, but she worried, nonetheless. Mothers do that."

I nodded in agreement.

"About a year after he'd left, the letters stopped coming. Anna was just frantic. Then a man from the war office came by to tell them that Arthur was missing in action. They didn't know if he had been taken prisoner or…" Her voice trailed off as she looked at Sarah, who was holding my hand tightly.

"That evening, Anna left the porch light on all night. Told Clem that she wouldn't turn it off until Arthur came home. A few days later I noticed that Ella Winter, down the road, had left her light on, too. So had the Moores. At twilight, I turned on a small lamp in my front window. It was the least I could do."

"How long did she have to leave the porch light on?" I asked, half dreading her response.

"Until she died," she answered in a soft voice. "Not long after Arthur had been reported missing, I went to pay a visit. When I turned to go, I noticed a big piece of tape over the switch to the porch light. Anna looked at it. 'No one touches that switch.' she said to me. 'Clem tried to turn it off one morning, but I stopped him. Told him I didn't care about the electricity.'"

Mrs. Harding looked at Sarah and continued. "A few years later, those little electric Christmas candles came out and the neighbors and I began burning them in our windows. We left them on for Arthur." She paused and then added, "And for all the others."

"The farmhouse still has its porch light on, doesn't it?" asked Sarah softly.

"Yes, dear." Mrs. Harding replied. "James lives in his parents' house now. The tape is still over the switch."

"Do you think that Arthur might come back someday?" asked Sarah quietly, her face full of worry.

"He might," Mrs. Harding said quietly.

"But he'd be very old, wouldn't he?" said Sarah.

That evening after supper, I heard noises in the attic and felt the cool draft that always meant someone had left the door at the top of the stairs open.

"Who's up there?" I called.

"Just me," Sarah's muffled voice responded.

She came down the stairs with one of our electric candles in her hand.

"I know it isn't Christmas yet, but I really want to put this in my window," she said, with a look that was at once hopeful and resolute.

"For Arthur?" I asked.

"Well, sort of," Sarah said. "But mostly for Kate. Maybe she's lost and just needs a light to guide her home."

I could not say no.

After I tucked her in, I stood in the doorway and looked at the candle.

Two weeks later, Kate returned—followed by three kittens. Where she'd been, we would never know. We were just glad to have her back.

"Can we leave the light on?" asked Sarah as we settled Kate into her basket. I nodded. We would leave our candle glowing. For Arthur. And for all the others.

House on the Lake

Mike Royko

$\sim\!\!\infty\!\!\sim$

When the two of them started spending weekends at the quiet Wisconsin lake, they were young and had little money. Her relatives let them use a tiny cottage in the wooded hollow a mile or so from the water.

He worked odd hours, so often they wouldn't get there until after midnight on a Friday. But if the mosquitoes weren't out, they'd go for a moonlight swim, then rest with their backs against a tree and sip wine and talk about their future.

One summer the young man bought an old motorboat. They'd ride along the shoreline, looking at the houses and wondering what it would be like to have a place on the water. He'd just shake his head; those houses cost more than he could ever afford.

Years passed. They had kids, and they didn't go to the little cottage as often. Finally her relatives sold the place.

Then he got lucky in his work, making more money than he ever dreamed they'd have. Remembering those weekends, they went back and bought a home on the water. A cedar house surrounded by big old trees, where the land sloped gently down to the shore. It was perfect.

They hadn't known summers could be that good. In the mornings he'd go fishing before it was light. She'd sleep until the birds woke her. Then he'd make breakfast, and they'd eat omelettes on the deck.

They got to know the chipmunks, the squirrels, and a woodpecker who took over their biggest tree. They got to know the grocer, the butcher who smoked his own bacon, the farmer who sold them vine-ripened tomatoes.

The best part of their day was dusk. She loved sunsets. They'd always stop to watch the sun go down, changing the color of the lake from blue, to purple, to silver, and then to black. One evening he made up a small poem:

The sun rolls down
Like a golden tear
Another day,
Another day
Gone.

She told him that it was sad, but that she liked it.

What she didn't like was October, even with its beautiful colors and evenings spent in front of the fireplace. She was a summer person. The cold wind wasn't her friend.

In November they would store the boat, take down the hammock, lock everything tight and drive back to the city. She'd always sigh as they left.

Finally spring would come, and when they knew the ice on the lake was gone, they'd be back. She'd throw open the doors and windows and let in the fresh air. Then she'd go out and greet the chipmunks and the woodpeckers.

Every summer seemed better than the last. The sunsets seemed more spectacular. And more precious.

Then one weekend he went alone to close the place down for the winter.

He worked quickly, trying not to let himself think that this particular chair had been her favorite, that the hammock had been her Christmas gift to him, that the house on the lake had been his gift to her.

He didn't work quickly enough. He was still there at sunset. It was a great burst of orange, the kind she had loved best.

He tried, but he couldn't watch it alone. Not through tears. So he turned his back on it, went inside, drew the draperies, locked the door, and drove away.

Later there would be a For Sale sign out front. Maybe a couple that loved to quietly watch sunsets together would like it. He hoped so.

I pray heaven to bestow the best of blessings on this house and all that shall hereafter inhabit it. May none but honest and wise men ever rule under this roof.

LETTER TO ABIGAIL ADAMS, NOVEMBER 2, 1800

Back Home

Emma Steward

❧

As a child, I lived some distance back in the woods. The road wandered aimlessly, like a writhing snake among huckleberry bushes and briers, along a sloping hillside where mountain laurel and honeysuckle blooms scented the air in late spring. It passed beside a field, which was enclosed with a barbed wire fence. Black Betty, our cow, was pastured there. Growing profusely along the fence were large lavender violets.

The spot where the road grew tired of winding and I got tired of walking was always the same. The huge boxwood bushes stood tall and graceful, as though they were soldiers guarding a humble little shack. The closest place to heaven—my home.

There was a two-story frame dwelling, always politely asking for a fresh coat of whitewash. It had a tin roof, painted as red as a strawberry, that rattled when the wind blew. A wisteria vine was tightly clinging to the front-porch columns, and a rusty screen door shrieked loudly when it was opened.

The floor was bare except for several scatter rugs my grandma had crocheted with a buttonhook. The ceilings were high and draped with a few cobwebs. The mantel was decorated with a seven-day alarm clock that had been on vacation for years. A kerosene lamp, its globe black from smoke, stood atop a dresser in the corner.

To the chimney was attached an old cast-iron heater, cracked down the side, which gave us comfortable warmth in cold weather. There was also a box of neatly sawed oak wood.

During the summer we waved a palm leaf fan to stir up a little breeze.

However, the second floor was air-conditioned rather well by a balm of Gilead tree that swayed with the wind and circulated a gentle breeze through our upstairs windows.

We ate in a little kitchen, which was set up out in the backyard away from the main house. The kitchen was like an icebox in the winter and a furnace in the summer.

We had an ugly old black cookstove, a huge square table usually covered with a bright floral-patterned oilcloth, and some round-back wooden chairs. A bucket of water from the moss-covered well in the backyard was placed on a little table by the stove, and a coconut shell dipper hung beside the bucket. Electricity hadn't found its way to our part of the country yet.

But our food was good. Nothing can quite compare to homemade biscuits, fried ham sizzling in redeye gravy, cabbage floating in ham grease, or butter cake with homemade chocolate icing. My mother would stand on the kitchen porch and call out when the meals were ready.

I spent a lot of time on the barrel-stave hammock in the backyard under the old gnarled trees. I would swing for hours in the fresh air and sunshine and become lost in pleasant reverie. That was my idea of recreation. I didn't know what it was to be lonely.

Mama was a delightful person. She was tall, stately, and slender, with warm brown eyes. Her long black hair was pinned in a bun at the nape of her neck. She was always busy cooking meals, churning cream, feeding chickens, washing clothes on an old scrub board, or drawing water with a windlass and rope from a fifty-foot well. But she found time to rock and cuddle me and sew for my dollies.

Daddy walked behind a mule, a horse, and a double plow all day, turning up fresh ground and plowing under old dead grass and broom straw. There were earthy smells everywhere. In the distance a crow would caw, and Daddy would mimic the crow's cry to frighten him away.

After supper sometimes we'd walk out to a neighbor's house, or else we'd just sit and talk or play the hand-cranked Victrola. Life was simple for us, but it was good.

Since those days, the world has changed a great deal—and so have I. With all our progress, though, love is still the greatest force on earth. It was love that made a humble country home seem like heaven.

What Is a Hom

It is the laughter of a child.
The song of a mother.
The strength of a father.
Home is the first school
And the first church where
They learn about a loving God.
Lord, this humble house we'd keep
Sweet with play and calm with sleep.
Help us so that we may give
Beauty to the lives we live.
Let Thy love and let Thy grace
Shine upon our dwelling place.

EDGAR A. GUEST

Porch Swing

Brenda A. Christensen

*was six months pregnant with our first child when we bought our first house—our very own home.

It was small and its early twentieth-century charm didn't hit me the first time we looked at it. The heat of August was aggravating my morning sickness, and the mosquitoes were on the offensive.

My husband liked it immediately. We were brought back when the real estate company held an open house. After dragging both our families through it, I changed my mind. Suddenly I saw the hundreds of flowers surrounding the entire yard, including the flower box that was actually the front wall of the front porch.

There was a giant maple tree, which must have witnessed every storm our small city had ever encountered and had still managed to hold its own. The enormous windows, though stained with years of tobacco smoke and layers of paint, drew me in further, as did the two window seats I had longed for as a young girl to sit in, dream, wish, or write in my diary. It would be perfect for my little girl.

But the thing that convinced me was the porch swing. It was all I had requested as we combed the city for a house: No porch for a swing, no deal. I had such fond memories of sitting on my grandparents' swing. All this place needed was a white picket fence, and we were set.

Our baby girl was born and our house seemed to be coming along—it did need some work done—and we spent much of our time outside as the weather began to warm. Walking around the block, playing chase in the grass, and, of course, swinging on the porch occupied much of our day.

Countless times I rocked her to sleep on that swing, and my second daughter as well.

We learned our ABC's and other charming songs and rhymes, including some we made up. The swing was frequently sticky from the popsicles melting in our hands on hot summer evenings. We played and swung wildly. We watched the traffic go by and the moon drift through the branches of the maple tree as we rocked softly. I sat on that swing and watched my girls play in the yard, jump in the leaves, and run through the sprinkler. I was in heaven.

From the day we bought our little "doll house," as our realtor referred to it, we were planning to sell it. My husband and I worked so hard to make necessary repairs and update the decorations. After five years and two children, we had outgrown our home. The time came to move out into the country, where I had always dreamed of raising my children. All I could do was cry the whole day.

We went back to the house one more time to make one final go-round, to eat one last quick meal in the old place, to enjoy one last sit in the swing.

I think the last five years of my life in that house flashed before me at that point, sort of like some people say it does before they near death. I cried so hard I could barely see to leave. We all waved good-bye and drove away with tearstained faces.

It had been over two months and I hadn't driven by, even once, until recently. I really wanted to visit the elderly neighbor lady whom I had befriended.

When I pulled up there was a young woman, about my age when I had my girls, sitting on my old porch swing and playing with her toddler behind the flowers I had planted earlier this spring. I hollered hello to her as I knocked on the neighbor's door.

I couldn't take my eyes off them. Nor could I hold back the tears that began streaming down my face. My friend wasn't home, and I was tempted to go over and introduce myself to the woman, but I decided not to since I knew I couldn't dry my eyes long enough to so much as say my name.

So I got into my car and pulled away, watching them play on the front porch through my rearview mirror.

I cried in sadness for my loss, and I cried in happiness for their gain. I cried in joy for the fate of my porch swing—making happy memories, as I am sure that it did before me, and as I have now seen that it will continue to do without me.

A porch is a hospitable soul. It welcomes guests of all degrees in a more cordial manner than the inside of a house ever knows. A porch comes halfway to meet a guest with outstretched hands, and bids him a lingering good-by when he must go.

DOROTHY SCARBOROUGH

This Is a Home Where Children Live

Judith Bond

You may not find things all in place,
Friend, when you enter here.
But we're a home where children live,
We hold them very dear.
And you may find small fingerprints
And smudges on the wall.
When the kids are gone, we'll clean them up,
Right now we're playing ball.
For there's one thing of which we're sure,
These children are on loan.
One day they're always underfoot,
Next thing you know, they're grown.
That's when we'll have a well-kept house,
When they're off on their own.
Right now, this is where children live,
A loved and lived-in home.

Lavender Memories

Sandra Picklesimer Aldrich and Bobbie Valentine

As Cotha Prior strolled past the new shop that sold body lotions and soaps, the lavender-wrapped bars displayed in the window caught her attention. Her daughter, Monica, would like those. Once inside, Cotha picked up the closest bar and held it to her nose. The fragrance carried her back to her childhood.

She remembered Margie, the little girl in her fifth grade class who always was poorly dressed and whose bathing habits were—well, not one of her regular habits. Even at that young age, Cotha knew how important the opinions of her friends were, so although she felt sorry for Margie, she couldn't risk being friends with her.

Then one afternoon, as young Cotha colored in the states on her homework worksheet, she casually mentioned Margie to her mother, who stopped in the middle of stirring the stew to ask, "What's her family like?"

Cotha didn't look up. "Oh, really poor. I guess," she answered.

"Well, it sounds as though she needs a friend," Mrs. Burnett said. "Why don't you invite her to spend Friday night with you?"

Cotha looked up quickly then. "You mean here? Spend the night with me? But, Mom...she smells."

"Cotha Helen." Her mother's use of both names meant the situation was settled. There was nothing to do but invite Margie home. The next morning Cotha hesitantly whispered the invitation at the end of recess while her friends were hanging up their jackets and combing their hair. Margie looked suspicious, so Cotha added, "My mother said it's okay. Here's a note from my mother to give to yours."

So two days later they rode the school bus home while Cotha tried to ignore the surprised looks on her friends' faces at the sight of the two of them together. Had two fifth grade girls ever been quieter? Cotha thought of other times when she'd been invited to spend the night with a friend, how they would talk and giggle all the way to their stop.

Finally Cotha gave a determined little huff and said to Margie, "I've got a cat. She's going to have kittens."

Margie's eyes lit up. "Oh, I like cats." Then she frowned, as though recalling a painful memory, and added, "But my dad doesn't."

Cotha didn't know what to say then, so she feigned interest in something outside the school bus window. Both girls were silent until the bus rolled to a stop in front of the white house with the green shutters.

Mrs. Burnett was in the kitchen. She greeted Cotha and Margie warmly and gestured toward the table, which was set with two glasses of milk and banana bread. "Why don't you girls have a little snack while I tend to dinner?"

When the banana bread was finished, Mrs. Burnett handed each child identical paper-doll books and blunted scissors. Dressing the paper women in shiny dresses gave them something in common to talk about. By the time they washed their hands for dinner, they were chatting enthusiastically about school.

After the dishes were done, Mrs. Burnett said, "Time to take a bath before bed, girls." Then she held out scented soaps wrapped in lavender paper. "Since this is a special night, I thought you might like to use fancy soaps," she said. "Cotha, you first, and I'll wash your back for you."

Then it was Margie's turn. If she was nervous about having an adult bathe her, she didn't show it. As the tub filled, Mrs. Burnett poured in a double capful of her own guarded bubble bath. "Don't you just love bubble bath, Margie?" she asked, as though assuming that the child bathed in such luxury every day.

She turned to pull Margie's grimy dress over her head, then said, "I'll look away as you take the other things off; but be careful climbing into the tub. That brand of bubble bath makes it slippery."

Once Margie was settled into the warm water, Mrs. Burnett knelt down and soaped the wet washcloth heavily before rubbing it over the child's back.

"Oh, that feels good," Margie said.

Mrs. Burnett chatted about how quickly Cotha and Margie were growing and what lovely young women they were already. Repeatedly she soaped the washcloth and scrubbed Margie's gray skin until it shone pink.

The whole time Cotha was thinking, Oh, how can she do that? Margie is so dirty. But Mrs. Burnett continued to scrub cheerfully; then she washed Margie's hair several times. Once Margie was out of the tub, Mrs. Burnett dried her back and dusted her thin shoulders with scented talcum. Then, since Margie had brought no nightclothes, Mrs. Burnett pulled one of Cotha's clean nightgowns over Margie's shining head.

After tucking both girls under quilts, Mrs. Burnett leaned over to gently kiss them good night. Margie beamed. As Mrs. Burnett whispered, "Good night, girls," and turned out the light, Margie pulled the clean sheets to her nose and breathed deeply. Then she fell asleep almost immediately.

Cotha was amazed that her new friend could fall asleep so quickly; she was used to talking and giggling for a long time with her other friends. To the sound of Margie's gentle breathing, Cotha stared at the shadows on the wall, thinking about all her mother had done. During Margie's bath, Mrs. Burnett had never once said anything to embarrass the girl, and she'd never even commented about how grimy the tub was afterward. She had just scrubbed it out, quietly humming the whole time. Somehow Cotha knew her mother had washed more than Margie's dingy skin.

All these years later, the adult Cotha stood in the store, the fragrant lavender soap still in her hand, wondering where Margie was now. Margie had never again mentioned Cotha's mother's ministrations, but Cotha had noticed a marked difference in the girl. Not only did Margie start coming to school clean and neatly-dressed on the outside, but she had an inner sparkle that perhaps came from knowing someone cared. For the rest of the school year, Cotha and Margie played at recess and ate lunch together. When Margie's family moved away at the end of the school year, Cotha never heard from her again. But she knew they had both been influenced by her mother's behavior.

Cotha smiled, then picked up a second bar of the lavender soap. She'd send that one to her mother, along with a letter thanking her mom for what she had given all those years ago—not only to Margie, but to Cotha, as well.

Nesting

Faith Andrews Bedford

Last month I hung an old rag rug over my porch railing to dry. A few minutes later, a little sparrow began pulling at the fringe, finding the soft cotton threads perfect for its nesting needs.

Birds are opportunists. In seeking to make strong yet comfortable nests for their young, they do not hesitate to use materials from nature—grasses, moss, twigs; and from man—yarn, rags, paper napkins. The straw I used to mulch my asparagus quickly becomes a nest maker's delight. And the string I use to tie up the hollyhocks is often shredded by nesting birds.

Early this morning, on my way to the garden, I noticed that the first bluebird fledglings of the season had flown from the nesting box. I raised the top of the little house on the fence post and carefully lifted out the old nest. Bluebirds claim a nesting box for their own and return to it year after year. We've discovered that if we clear out the nest as soon as the fledglings have flown, their parents may build another and raise as many as three families each summer.

Whenever I clean out the dryer's lint trap or brush our cat, I take the resulting fluff deep into the woods and scatter it on bushes in the hopes that birds will find it useful. It is my thank-you to them for filling these same woods with song.

As I clean out the various nesting boxes we have around our place, I sometimes do see evidence that things I've set out for birds have been incorporated into nests. But just as often, I find surprises.

Last year a little jenny wren found her way into my shed and built a nest in a raspberry bucket. When July came and it was time to pick berries, I got the bucket down and pulled out a nest filled with green ribbons, the kind that curl when pulled along a scissors' blade.

The titmice in the birdhouse by the barn incorporated some thin orange streamers into their nest. The long paper strands look as though they came from a cheerleader's pom-pom. And some ruby finches made a nest in a basket of impatiens on the porch. Their nestling had a glorious canopy of red flowers for a roof. I took great care not to disturb them when I watered the flowers. Perhaps, I thought, they'll just believe that I am a small rainstorm. When the last baby had fledged, I removed the nest and found that the finches had woven into it faded cellophane "grass" from a child's Easter basket.

My husband is amused that I save dryer fluff and bits of yarn for the birds. I shall have to show him this bluebird nest.

Cradling it gently in my hand, I head back to the house to start dinner. As I pass through the front hall, I catch my reflection in the oval mirror that hangs there. I found it in New York City when my son was a baby. I had taken Drew for a walk in his carriage and, on our way home, I spotted the mirror propped up against a streetlight at the bottom of an old brownstone's steps. I stopped short. I remembered that it was "Big Junk Night" in Manhattan, but couldn't believe that someone was throwing away this wonderful old mirror. The lady who lived in the house helped me place it crosswise on the pram. Holding it steady, I carefully pushed Drew the three blocks home.

Thus began my career as a lover of "found objects." When our drugstore closed after ninety-four years of business, the owner put out a box of old apothecary jars. Most were cracked, but some still had their original gilt labels. I carried two home and, with directions from the clerk at the hardware store. turned them into small table lamps. Later, an old treadle sewing machine, minus the cabinet, became a table base. A faded blanket was washed and given a new cover, then tied with yarn. Fifteen years later, it still keeps us warm.

When we bought our first house, I haunted thrift shops and combed tag sales. I made pillows out of usable bits of tattered quilts and sewed curtains from old sheets, the once-brilliant colors of which had faded to soft, muted shades.

"You certainly are a nester," my mother remarked one day as she helped me slipcover an armchair that a neighbor had put out for the trash man.

Her words come back to me as I gaze at my reflection in the hall mirror. "One man's trash is another man's treasure," I had replied to her then. Now, looking down at the nest in my hand, I wonder: Perhaps that should be rephrased as "One creature's trash is another creature's treasure."

The dryer buzz suddenly signals the end of a load. I put the warm clothes in a basket. Then I pull out the lint trap and brush off a handful of fluff. After dinner, I'll take it into the woods. It's still early in the season—perhaps the bluebirds will find it.

BLESSINGS OF THE HOME
The crown of the home is godliness;
The beauty of the home is order;
The glory of the home is hospitality;
The blessing of the home is contentment.

HENRY VAN DYKE

Gently Swinging

Kimber Annie Engstrom

Gently swinging. Quietly creaking. Back and forth. Back and forth. Here I sit. Here I listen. Listening to the music of the front porch swing.

The weathered wood all laced with stains speaks clearly. It talks of cold snow, warm hugs, and hot summer nights. It tattles of spilled lemonade, whispers of tipped teacups, and shares of precious tears. This is a sacred place. A place where conversation and emotion grace the air. A place where dreams are free to dance. A place where finding oneself is possible.

Gently swinging. Quietly creaking. I keep listening to the music of the front porch swing.

I hear it speak of hands. Many hands. Smooth hands. Wrinkled hands. Muddy hands. Gloved hands. Helping hands. Holding hands. Hands in love. It is here I fold my hands, and it is here I talk to God. He holds my hands, and it is here that He talks to me.

Gently swinging. Quietly creaking. Back and forth. Back and forth. Here I sit. Here I listen. Listening to the music of the front porch swing.

Moments Set Apart

Find a place where your thoughts can soar, your spirit can rest, your mind can slip into a realm of peace and abandon. Let yourself be surprised by the common things that God sets afire for you: the morning sun on a piece of carpet, the silky fur of a kitten, the lingering scent of a spouse or child who has just left for the day. Give God thanks for every moment thus set apart. Ask Him to fill your working (and sleeping) dreams with beauty, light, and vision.

KATHERINE STEWARD

Leaving Home

John Trent

High school was over, and I'd been up almost all night, first saying good-bye to my few remaining high school friends and then packing for college myself. Now I sat at our old kitchen table with my mother, enjoying her famous pancakes one last time before climbing into my jam-packed car. As I sat at that table, a flood of emotions hit me.

My mother had purchased the table when I was five years old. It sat next to a large kitchen window, with a commanding view of the front yard. For more than a decade, it served as the unofficial meeting place of the Trent family. In grade school, I can remember sitting there at countless dinners. There would be us three boys laughing and chattering about our day, my mother and grandmother scurrying back and forth to keep bottomless plates filled, and my grandfather quietly presiding over the chaos.

In high school, that table became the place where I could sit with my mother anytime, day or night. There she would patiently listen to whatever "crisis" I was having in school or in dating. That old table proudly displayed birthday cards as we grew older and solemnly bore the flowers we brought home from the funeral home the day my grandfather was laid to rest.

Over the years, more chairs began to empty. My older brother, Joe, married and began a home of his own. My grandmother went to live with my aunt, and my twin brother, Jeff, left for a different college. Now it was down to just Mom and me, sitting at that table one last time.

I can remember how well I thought she was handling that morning. No tears. No dip in her ever-present smile. Just that nonstop encouragement that has calmed my fears since I was a child and always made me feel like

I could accomplish anything I set my mind to. Like driving a thousand miles by myself to a new college and making a new start without knowing a single person at an out-of-state school.

I finished breakfast, hugged the best mom in the world, and confidently strode to my '64 forest-green Volkswagen. Every square inch was crammed with "important stuff" for college—everything from my legendary record collection to my new, seldom-used razor. I jumped inside the car, fired up the engine, and drove off with a wave and a smile. I was on my way! Nothing was going to stop me now! Nothing, that is, except driving into the rising sun that quickly made me realize I'd forgotten one thing—my sunglasses on the night stand.

I turned the car around, drove back into the driveway, and walked in to find my mother still sitting at the kitchen table…crying. All morning she had kept a stiff upper lip, managing to hold her emotions in check at seeing her last son leave home. But when I walked back in the door unexpectedly, all that changed. There was an awkward silence, and then we both lost it. We sat at that table, crowded with memories, hugged each other, and cried and cried.

I can't explain exactly what happened that sun-splashed morning in the kitchen, but our relationship changed. There was no less love, no less caring, but somehow we both knew that this would be the last time I would sit down at that old kitchen table as a child.

Heritage of Faith

Sally J. Knower

❦

*T*he old rocker cracked and popped as Jenny set it in motion with a push of her hand. The springs poked wire heads through the faded horsehair covering. Even in the dimly lit attic, she could see the wood was scarred and the varnish worn away. She tugged the relic to the stairwell and slid it, one step at a time, carefully balancing the awkward weight against her watermelon belly. At the bottom of the stairs she kneaded the muscles at her lower back.

"Jenny Lester, what did you do? You shouldn't have brought the chair down by yourself," Audrea Lester scolded.

"I'm all right, Mother Lester."

The baby squirmed and kicked its objections. She laughingly rubbed the rebel pushing from within. "You just wait. Someday I'll rock you in Grandmother Lester's chair."

Clara and Harry Lester bought the chair shortly after their wedding in 1889. They moved it by horse and wagon from the secondhand store in Lincoln, Nebraska, to their farm outside of Fairbury. Harry refinished the wood. Clara upholstered its back and seat with fashionable horsehair material. Only special, come-into-the-parlor company like Reverend Jorganson used it until the babies came. Then Clara niched it between the wood stove and table in the all-purpose kitchen.

As she soothed babies with its cadence, the chair became hers. She'd touch down between stirring the stew and slopping the sows they raised. Tea towel harnesses secured toddlers to the chair while she canned and preserved.

She anxiously shuttled the chair to and fro when scarlet fever made her third child delirious. "God," she railed, "if you're really out there, help my little one." When healing came, tears of relief sprinkled her apron. "God, I believe you are real. You heard me. Thank you for saving my son. He is yours now, Lord, and so am I."

The chair became her altar and her podium. She tucked her feet up on it and leaned toward the lamp to read her Bible, then faced it into the corner to form a prayer closet.

The chair kept rhythm with the songs she sang, from quiet lullabies to joyous hallelujahs. It fairly jumped with her tapping toe when Harry squeezed music from his concertina.

Clara darned socks for her growing sons and snapped beans while seated on its broad cushion. When grandchildren came, they teethed on the chair's arms.

She sat in the chair and captivated her family with true stories of adventure like the day the rabid dog ran through the farmyard without biting anyone, or when the tornado blew the shingles from the roof and no one was hurt. She told how David slew Goliath with one smooth stone, and how Daniel survived a night in a den full of hungry lions.

The chair sat by the four-poster bed as Harry wrestled with cancer. Clara sat vigilant at his side and held his hand. After he died she pulled the chair close to the stove and wondered if she would ever feel warm again.

Taxes grew but funds didn't. Clara's resources diminished. The farm had to be sold. She rocked and watched as, piece by piece, equipment and furnishings were auctioned. It was like tearing strips from her life to see them go. Clara kept only the chair. She took it with her when she went to live with her youngest son, Robert, and his wife, Audrea.

Audrea made room for the chair. It looked incongruous beside French provincial in the townhouse. She tried to make Clara welcome, but Clara felt about as comfortable as a corn in a Sunday shoe.

Then Jimmy was born. The last little grandson to rock in her arms and tug at her hair. As he grew she shrank. Low oxygen days fogged her mind. Only her God and her chair remained familiar. Alien noises—fire engines, horns, and squealing brakes—interrupted her sleep. Clara endured restless hours wrapped in a quilt, rocking, praying, and waiting to go home.

After her death the worn old chair was relegated to Jimmy's room. He was delighted to have it. He used it to hunt tigers. He drove horses from the chariot it formed. He did homework in it as he kept time to his raucous radio. He dreamed dreams and planned his future within its circle.

The chair developed a popping sound under the weight of a boy turned man.

When he went away to college his old room became a guest room and den. The rocker disappeared.

A freckled coed caught Jimmy's fancy and he courted

her his senior year. They married. Jenny worked while he went to seminary. He got the call to his first church hand-in-hand with the call to fatherhood.

Their first child grew and stretched beneath Jenny's heart. "I wish we had my grandmother's chair," Jimmy said as he lightly touched Jenny's bulging front. "You could rock our son in it."

"Or daughter," Jenny countered.

"That old rocker was special. I felt so proud when the chair was given to me. I wonder where it is now."

"Mother Lester," Jenny asked the next time she saw her mother-in-law, "whatever became of the rocking chair Jimmy used to have in his room?"

"It's in the attic," Audrea answered.

"I'd like to see it. I have an idea."

"Come on, I'll show it to you. It's in bad shape. You can see where the stuffing is coming out and the wood is marred," Audrea said as she switched on the attic light.

Jenny rubbed her hand across the back of the rocker. "The scars aren't deep. They just add character. It will take work but I think it can be fixed. Can I try? I'd like to surprise Jimmy. It would be a terrific anniversary gift."

"You can if you want to. In fact, you can work on it in Jimmy's old room."

As Mother Lester readied the spare room Jenny

brought the chair down from the attic. She was so anxious to begin.

Beautiful oak came out of hiding as Jenny stripped the old surface and sanded it smooth. The wood glowed softly under new varnish. Jenny tied down the old springs. They were snug and comfortable under the new coverings. It looked very handsome with its clean claw feet and trimly tucked back.

On celebration day Jenny draped a ribbon, Miss America style, across the chair's shoulders.

"What are you up to, Jenny Lester?" her husband asked as she led him up the stairs to his old room. "Your grin gives you away."

"Close your eyes while I open the door. Better put your hands over them too." He dutifully covered up. "Now, no peeking."

"You act like an excited little kid," Jimmy chuckled. "Are you sure you're old enough to have my son?"

"Okay," she said after positioning him in front of the rocker. "You can look. Happy anniversary."

"Grandmother Lester's rocker! Oh, honey, it's wonderful," he exclaimed as he draped Jenny's torso with the Miss America ribbon.

That evening at home, next to the full-sized bed, Jimmy rocked Jenny on his lap.

"You'd better let me up," Jenny said as the chair cracked and popped. "It's complaining."

"No you don't," Jimmy said as Jenny tried to rise.

"You aren't going anywhere. It's not complaining. It's just talking to us."

"So it has a voice of its own, does it? It almost has a life of its own." Jenny mused.

"It certainly has a heritage," Jimmy said. "When our son is born I am going to tell him about the heritage of faith that began with Grandmother Lester and came down four generations to him."

"Or her," Jenny countered sleepily.

What Is Home?
It is the laugh of a baby,
the songs of a mother,
the strength of a father,
Warmth of loving hearts,
light from happy eyes, kindness,
loyalty, comradeship,
Where joy is shared and sorrow eased,
Where even the teakettle sings from happiness.
That is home.

ERNESTINE SCHUMANN HEINK

Homeward Journey

Janet Paschal

It was a warm Saturday afternoon. A Carolina breeze was steadily moving through the long grass and the proud, full branches. I was driving home, back to the little corner of the world where I grew up. I was en route to a modest house on a corner lot bordered by pine trees, vegetable gardens, and neighbors who still bake casseroles for each other.

I was thinking that when I arrive, my dad—most likely out by his newly painted tractor—will head across the freshly mown lawn. He'll hug me long and hard until the back door slams. My mom will reach for me, smiling, and announce, "I've a fresh pitcher of iced tea. Who's ready for a glass?" In a few moments my nephew will bound across the road, dog in tow.

I knew I'd spend the next few days with people who love me unconditionally. The awards I have or haven't received are insignificant. My career, whether rocketing or plummeting, is rarely mentioned. They just care that I come. They just want me.

What really matters is home. This is the stuff I am made of. This is what is important to me.

We are all on a homeward journey. God patiently plans our routes and polices our perils. He watches us maneuver through detours and treacherous places. He even sees us make an occasional wrong turn, then keep going anyway.

But always He waits. Long ago He paved the way and marked the direction for us to come to Him. He

prepared a place of rest that is beyond the reaches of our imaginations—a welcome center built by His own hand.

He doesn't care what religious label we bear. Our nationality or net worth won't matter. He just cares that we come. He just wants us home.

Make two homes for thyself. . . .
One actual home. . .
and another spiritual home,
which thou art to carry with thee always.

AUTHOR UNKNOWN

Home Sweet Home

I read within a poet's book
A word that starred the page,
"Stone walls do not a prison make,
Nor iron bars a cage."
Yes, that is true, and something more:
You'll find where'er you roam,
That marble floors and gilded walls
Can never make a home.
But every house where love abides
And friendship is a guest,
Is surely home…home, sweet home,
For there the heart can rest.

Henry Van Dyke

Acknowledgments

A diligent search has been made to trace original ownership, and when necessary, permission to reprint has been obtained. If I have overlooked giving proper credit to anyone, please accept my apologies. Should any attribution be found to be incorrect, the publisher welcomes written documentation supporting correction for subsequent printings. For material not in the public domain, grateful acknowledgment is given to the publishers and individuals who have granted permission for use of their material.

Acknowledgments are listed by story title in the order they appear in the book. For permission to reprint any of the stories, please request permission from the original source listed below.

"Teacups of Love" by Nancy Jo Sullivan. Taken from *Moments of Grace*, by Nancy Jo Sullivan © 2000. Used by permission of Multnomah Publishers.

"Old Doors" by Carla Muir. Used by permission of the author.

"A Single Crocus" by Joan Wester Anderson. Taken from *Where Wonders Prevail*, by Joan Wester Anderson, copyright © 1996 by Joan Wester Anderson. Used by permission of Ballantine Books, a division of Random House, Inc.

"The Spirit of Hospitality" by Emilie Barnes. Taken from *The Spirit of Loveliness*, by Emilie Barnes. Copyright © 1999 by Harvest House Publishers. Eugene, OR. Used by permission.

"A Light in the Window" by Faith Andrews Bedford. Her short stories have been published in numerous magazines; her column "Kids in the Country" appears in *Country Living*. Her most recent book is *The Sporting Art of Frank W. Benson* (Godine, 2000).

"House on the Lake" by Mike Royko. Reprinted with special permission from the *Chicago Sun-Times*, Inc. © 2001 and with permission from the December 1997 *Reader's Digest*.

"Back Home" by Emma Steward. © 1980. This story was first published in *Seek* magazine by Standard Publishing in 1981 and then in *Stories for a Woman's Heart*, Multnomah Publishers (Sisters, OR) in 1999. Used by permission of the author. She can be reached at 5501 Good Hope Rd., Lanexa, VA 23089.

"Porch Swing" by Brenda A. Christensen. Used by permission of the author. Brenda is a school-age childcare director, married, and the mother of two. She loves to garden and to sit in the barn loft looking out over the stars (until her front porch is built for a swing, of course).

"This Is a Home Where Children Live" by Judith Bond. © 1989. Used by permission of the author. Judith Bond is a poet and artist living in New York. She is the creator of *Books of Love* and other fine gift products featuring her poetry and artwork.

"Lavender Memories" by Sandra Picklesimer Aldrich and Bobbie Valentine. Reprinted from *Heartprints*. Copyright © 1999 by Sandra Picklesimer Aldrich and Bobbie Valentine. Used by permission of WaterBrook Press. Colorado Springs, CO. All rights reserved.

"Nesting" by Faith Andrews Bedford. Her short stories have been published in numerous magazines; her column "Kids in the Country" appears in *Country Living*. Her most recent book is *The Sporting Art of Frank W. Benson* (Godine, 2000).

"Gently Swinging" by Kimber Annie Engstrom. © 1999. Used by permission of the author.

"Leaving Home" by John Trent. Taken from *Love for All Seasons*, by John Trent © 1996. Used by permission of Moody Press. Chicago, IL.

"Heritage of Faith" by Sally J. Knower. © 1995. Used by permission of the author.

"Homeward Journey" taken from *The Good Road*, by Janet Paschal. © 1997. Used by permission of the author.